vegetarian
and
seafood
recipes

Issy Warrack with Estrelita van Rensburg

vegetarian
and
seafood
recipes

THE LOW-CARB WAY

Also by Estrelita van Rensburg and Issy Warrack

Eat Well or Die Slowly: Your Guide to Metabolic Health
Eat Your Way to Health: Recipes for Success

Wellness EQ® Publishers

The information in this book is provided to assist the reader in making informed choices about their diet. This book is not intended as a substitute for medical advice, and anybody changing their diet should consult their physician about the treatment implications of any underlying medical conditions.

Artwork

Molly Tyrrell

Photography and Illustrations

Gideon Sauer, Estrelita van Rensburg and Issy Warrack, iStock: 92206244, 118321359, 148792864, 155157907, 162403988, 182150336, 185296258, 464583605, 473426692, 474461060, 487138402, 497948923, 506918835, 523263890, 526491425, 536552541, 541123870, 618328002, 626516364, 642250416, 664213066, 691210680, 877057638, 901449184, 927898232 , 941858854-1, 942152278, 1056787448, 1084840800, 1130922737, 1145709175, 1156379587, 1162339809, 1203233192, 1203725513, 1216002630, 1225818440, 1300328157, 157565232, 610957954. Pixabay: 3251560_1920, 2031362_1280

Cover Design

Elisabeth Heissler Design

Interior Design

Elisabeth Heissler Design
Estrelita van Rensburg

ISBN (Paperback) 978-1-8381378-4-7

Visit us at www.wellnesseq.net

contents

introduction...9

drinks, sauces, pastes & seasonings................................. 19

Cafe Latte 21
Frothy Chai Latte 23
Turmeric Latte 25
Masala Seasoning 27
Fresh Tomato Sauce 29
Masala Paste 31
Aioli 33
Classic Pesto 35
Tomato and Olive Sauce 37
Raita 39

salads and light meals..41

Low-carb Bread 43
Quick Indian-style Snack 45
Herby Mushrooms on Butter-Fried Bread 47
Smoked Salmon with Creamy Horseradish 49
Avocado Salad 53
Marinated Olives 55
Tapas: Patatas Bravas 57
Fish Tapas 59
Goat's Cheese on Low-carb Bread 61
Asparagus with Salsa Verde 63

vegetables mains and sides 65

Vegetable Rice 67

Zoodles 69

Creamy Cauliflower Mash 71

Cabbage Stir Fry 73

Middle Eastern Butter Bean Stew 75

Pav Bhaji 77

Nut Roast 79

Indian Roasted Cauliflower 81

Roasted Peppers with Baby Tomatoes 83

eggs 85

French Toast 87

Tunisian Chakchouka 89

Classic Pissaladière 91

Quick Eggs Traybake 95

Anchovy and Egg Salad with Croutons 97

Smoked Salmon and Creamy Egg Pots 99

vegetables with cheese 101

Spicy Eastern Mediterranean Vegetable Bake 103

Creamy Radish Gnocchi with Olives and Gorgonzola 105

Aubergine Parmigiana 107

Faux Pasta with Brussels Sprouts topped with Cheese 109

Stuffed Peppers 111

Neapolitan Bake 113

Paneer Keema 115

Tandoori Paneer Tikka 117

Roasted Radishes 119

One-Pan Indian Cuisine 121

seafood 123

Paella 125

Creamy Crab Omelette 127

Spicy Mussels Rasam with Vegetable 131

Indian Fish Curry 133

Prawn (Shrimp) Chow Mein 135

Lobster Risotto 137

Prawn (Shrimp) Stir Fry with Pine Nuts 139

Fish Jalfrezi 141

Bouillabaisse 143

Cambodian Fish Amok 145

Hot and Sour Calamari (Squid) 147

Baked Sardines 149

White Fish with Herby Wine Sauce 151

Tuna Steaks with Olives and Saffron 153

Barbecued Trout 155

Mackerel Recheado 157

Acknowledgements 159

About the authors 161

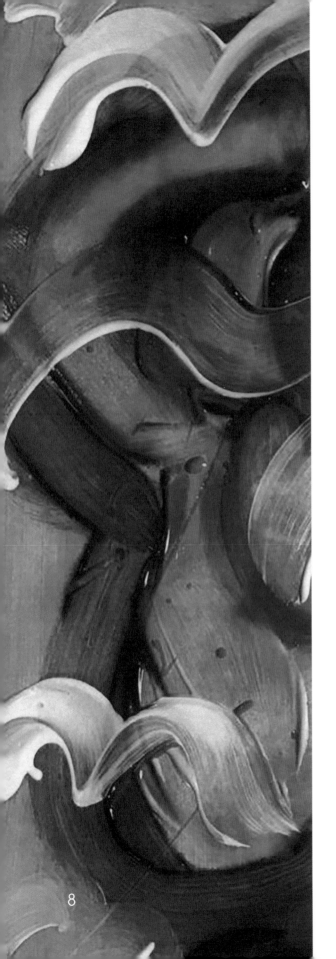

'Your diet is a bank account. Good food choices are good investments.'

BETHENNY FRANKEL

introduction

Why this book?

We are both passionate about good food – nutritious real food sourced from trusted local suppliers – and we have both been heavily influenced by our scrumptious foodie experiences on our travels. This book is a flavoursome journey through the Mediterranean countries, India and the Far East, inspired by our own experiences and supplemented by the expertise and generosity of friends who shared their countries' culinary delights and fresh preparation methods.

The reader will instantly see the emphasis we place on using fresh ingredients and, where possible, we highly recommend doing so to fully appreciate the true flavours of all the recipes. You will note that we also strongly advocate making your own sauces, pastes and seasonings. It will give you a truly authentic experience. Just taste the difference between a freshly made herby tomato sauce compared with that from a shop-bought can! You'll love it – and all of the recipes are quick and easy!

These recipes reflect our own successful low carbohydrate journey. We would love you to join us, whether you want to lose weight, reduce your meds for type 2 diabetes, get rid of brain fog, improve your heart health or improve your optimum health levels – in fact, just to generally feel on top of the world!

Come join us!

Healthy eating

To support all the metabolic processes in our body, we need to eat nutritious real food and not the heavily processed industrialised versions promoted by supermarkets worldwide. Our principal reason for writing this book was to provide recipes that use fresh locally sourced products to promote optimal health.

Essential nutrients are crucial to a person's good health and are divided into two categories: micronutrients and macronutrients. There are three macronutrients (fat, protein and carbohydrates) and many more micronutrients (vitamins and minerals). Of the three macronutrients, only protein and fat are essential. Our body cannot make protein and certain fatty acids; therefore, we need to obtain these macronutrients from eating animal or plant food sources.

Naturally occurring fats are

Despite what we have been told for decades, naturally occurring fats – saturated and all unsaturated fats as well as fatty acids – in both animal and plant sources (butter, avocados, olives and coconuts) are healthy. Naturally occurring healthy fats are required to absorb the essential fat-soluble vitamins A, D, E and K from our gut. For effective absorption, we need to eat full-fat products and not the 'low-fat' variety predominantly available in our supermarkets.

Omega-3, one of the family of polyunsaturated fats has anti-inflammatory properties and is very important for brain development and intelligence. The best dietary source of omega-3 is fatty fish. It is worth noting that plant-based foods do not contain the correct type of omega-3 that our body requires. Conversion of plant omega-3 (alpha-linolenic acid or ALA) to the types of omega-3 that we need (eicosapentaenoic acid or EPA and docosahexaenoic acid or DHA) is a very inefficient process. DHA is the most important omega-3 for optimal brain function, making up to 40 per cent of the total brain fat content. However, the expertly marketed industrially produced vegetable/seed oils, high in omega-6, are pro-inflammatory and should be avoided.

If we restrict animal food sources totally, the body is likely to become deficient in protein, certain essential fats and some vitamins and minerals.

Essential protein

All our cells and tissues contain protein. Proteins form the structural frames for our muscles, bones, organs, skin and hair. Inside every cell of the body, proteins form part of various functional elements, such as hormones, our immune system's antibodies and enzymes, all of which are involved in a wide range of metabolic interactions. It also provides a storage or carrier function within the body, e.g. the protein haemoglobin carries oxygen to all our cells. Protein is essential for the growth and repair of cells and the maintenance of good health. Since the body does not store excess protein, daily intake is essential to keep us strong and healthy.

Nutrient Type	Animal Foods	Plant Foods
Protein	highest quality, contains all amino acids	lack one or more amino acids
Vitamin A	retinol (active form)	β-carotene (precursor), only 3-28% converted to retinol
Vitamin D	D3: most efficient form	D2: less efficient form
Vitamin K	K2: better utilised in body	K1: poorly absorbed
Vitamin B12	good supply	not present
Omega-3 fatty acids	EPA: anti-inflammatory DHA: brain function and neurological development	ALA: very low conversion to active forms EPA and DHA
Iron	heme-iron: 6-8 times better absorbed than non-heme iron	non-heme iron: phytates and tannins in plants inhibit absorption
Zinc	very high concentration in oysters, meat and poultry	plant anti-nutrients inhibit absorption

Animal products such as meat, poultry, eggs, dairy and fish are complete sources of protein that contain all nine essential amino acids. Most plant sources lack essential amino acids, are less digestible than animal proteins, contain less protein per ounce than animal-based foods and are more prone to causing allergies and sensitivities. For vegetarians and vegans, soy is a popular plant-based source of protein, as it contains all the essential amino acids. However processed soy foods are no better for human health than any other highly processed foods, and they also carry the added risk of hormonal interference due to the phytoestrogens found in all forms of soy.

Grains contain plant proteins, the most infamous of which is gluten, a family of plant proteins found in wheat, rye, and barley. Gluten is extremely difficult to digest and can also damage the lining of the intestinal tract, causing inflammation and increased gut permeability (leaky gut). Leaky gut symptoms can include abdominal pain, chronic diarrhoea, constipation, bloating, headaches, brain fog, low mood and tiredness.

In addition to the importance of protein, many plant foods are indeed rich in minerals and vitamins. Not all these plant nutrients are available in the best format, allowing our body to absorb and utilise them efficiently. See the table above comparing animal and plant-based foods for the bioavailability of some of these essential nutrients.

Carbohydrates

Carbohydrates are the only non-essential macronutrient. After digestion in our gut, the basic metabolic component of all carbohydrates (sugar and starch) is glucose. Glucose stimulates the release of insulin, a hormone produced by our pancreas, which helps glucose enter our cells where it is used to produce energy. The second function of insulin is to store fat in our body. This happens when we eat too many carbohydrates – regrettably, the principal component of most processed foods sold in supermarkets.

Over time, if we continue to follow a high-carbohydrate diet, a significant proportion of the population will develop insulin resistance, which is the precursor to lifestyle diseases (obesity, type 2 diabetes, heart disease, dementia, cancer etc) that are so prevalent today.

So, what is the correct or ideal carbohydrate value that you should aim for? Each of us has a critical carbohydrate threshold. If you are predisposed to gaining weight, your insulin threshold will be lower, resulting in a more carbohydrate-sensitive disposition (i.e. low carbohydrate tolerance). When that occurs, you will start to gain weight and experience increased hunger, which in turn drives you to consume more carbohydrates (sugar and starch are truly addictive). It is a vicious circle.

net carbs range per 100g	Food examples per category
0-5g	coconut oil, coconut cream, double (heavy) cream, milk (full fat), Greek yoghurt, ricotta cheese, feta cheese, mozzarella cheese, paneer, Parmesan cheese, eggs, Brazil nuts, pecans, seafood, artichokes, turnips, spinach, avocado, lettuce, asparagus, cucumber, cabbage, cauliflower, celery, tomatoes, garlic (1-5 cloves), olives, mushrooms, courgettes (zucchini), kale, broccoli, green beans, Brussels sprouts, peppers, fennel, mangetout (snap peas), radishes, aubergine (eggplant), squash, red kidney beans, raspberries, blackberries
6-10g	pumpkin, beetroot, carrots, celeriac, butter beans, pine nuts, walnuts, almonds, butternut, chickpeas (garbanzo beans), peas, soybeans (cooked), orange, lemon, strawberries, blueberries
11-15g	leeks, parsnips, shallots, lentils (cooked), any bread (per slice), potatoes, onion/shallots, mango, apple, pear, peach
16-25g	sweet potatoes, sweet corn, quinoa (cooked), buckwheat, cereal, Weetabix, grapes, banana
26g+	rice, pasta, pizza (per slice), chocolate, cookies, oatmeal

There is no absolute daily net carbohydrate value that will suit every person, but we know from experience that most people who are not overweight nor suffering from lifestyle diseases consume, on average, not more than 50g of net carbohydrates daily. For some people, it can be higher – up to 100g or even 200g.

Vegetarians who cook with lentils and pulses will notice that these ingredients are excluded from our low-carb book. A serving of lentils has 15g of net carbs, which, if following a very low-carb diet, may exceed the daily net carb allowance. See the net carbohydrate content of commonly used food products in the table on the left.

Artificial sweeteners

We acknowledge that some people cannot initially accept the taste of unsweetened foods and, in those cases, we do suggest using your favourite sweetener. We have found that, with time, people come to love the taste of the foods in these recipes and no longer need to use sweeteners. Research has shown that artificial sweeteners are addictive in animals and that people who consume these products daily have a greater risk of developing insulin resistance and type 2 diabetes. In the herbs and spices section below, we include cinnamon, which can be used as a natural sweetener and may be an alternative for you.

Challenges of vegetarian and vegan diets

The bottom line is that both vegetable and plant-based diets can be highly restrictive and may create problems over time, including nutrient deficiencies and restricted eating patterns. Since a vegan diet excludes all forms of animal protein, including meat, fish, eggs, and dairy, people following this diet often turn to legumes and grains as a plant-based protein source. Legumes have high levels of antinutrients such as lectins and phytates, both of which can increase intestinal permeability, also called leaky gut.

Vegetables may contain high levels of naturally occurring antinutrient factors (including digestive enzyme inhibitors, tannins and phytates). These compounds have a variety of effects such as reducing the digestibility of food and the uptake of minerals such as iodine, iron, calcium and magnesium.

These diets typically have a high carbohydrate count and can promote the development of insulin resistance and associated diseases. It is possible to live a vegetarian lifestyle on a very low-carbohydrate or keto diet (20 grams of net carbohydrates per day), but the more restrictive the diet, the more challenging it is to achieve a low carbohydrate count while still eating food that contains all the essential nutrients.

It is important for those following a restrictive diet to regularly monitor their vitamin B12 and vitamin D levels as well as the presence of anaemia. High-quality supplements are essential to prevent deficiencies and associated symptoms.

Herbs and spices

Why have we chosen these particular herbs and spices? Great question! The answer is flavour enhancement – they add excitement and have added health benefits (shown below). What more could we want?

Allspice	anti-inflammatory	**Marjoram**	anti-inflammatory and antioxidant
Basil	powerful antioxidant	**Mint**	anti-inflammatory and good for digestion
Bay leaf	excellent source of β-carotene; use for flavouring	**Mustard**	nutrient-rich
Cardamom	anti-inflammatory	**Nutmeg**	powerful anti-inflammatory and antioxidant
Chilli	good source of antioxidants	**Paprika**	nutrient-rich
Chives	great flavouring, packed with vitamin K1	**Parsley**	rich in antioxidants
Cinnamon	loaded with antioxidants and a natural sweetener	**Peppercorns**	anti-inflammatory and high in antioxidants
Coriander (Cilantro)	rich in immune-boosting antioxidants	**Rosemary**	anti-inflammatory
Cumin	promotes good digestion	**Saffron**	high in antioxidants
Fennel	powerful antioxidant	**Sage**	assists hot flushes – use as an infusion
Fenugreek	strong antioxidant	**Salt**	add mineral salt for low-carb diet
Garam Masala	helps with digestion	**Star Anise**	optimises digestion
Garlic	good for heart health	**Tarragon**	nutrient-rich
Ginger	great for digestion	**Thyme**	powerful anti-inflammatory and antioxidant
Lemongrass	antioxidant and anti-inflammatory	**Turmeric**	anti-inflammatory

How to use this cookbook to monitor metabolic health

Our daily net carbohydrate intake is a good indicator of our metabolic health. To assist with this, we calculated the net carb value per serving for each recipe provided. These values are calculated by taking the carbohydrate value of a particular ingredient and then deducting its fibre content. For example, if an ingredient has 10g of carbohydrates and 4g of fibre, the net carb value is 6g. For each recipe, we visually display the net carb count using colour sensitive metabolic icons. You should aim to keep your total net carb intake per day as low as possible if you wish to improve your metabolic health.

Recipe icons indicating net carbohydrate values per serving

 0 – 5g/serving

 5 – 10g/serving

 11 – 15g/serving

 15 – 20g/serving

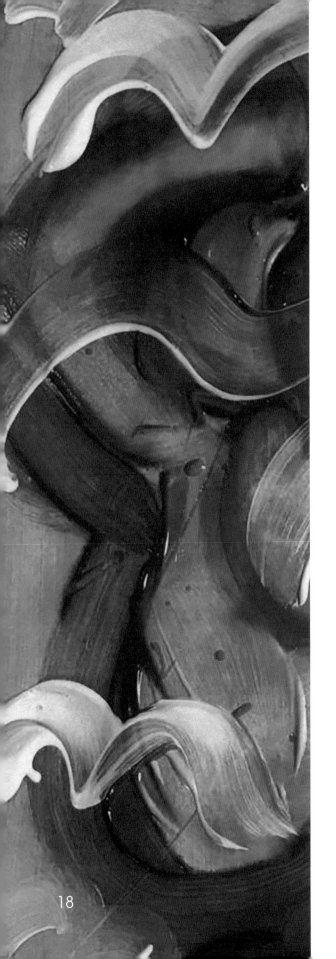

'When you start eating food without labels, you no longer need to count calories.'

AMANDA KRAFT

drinks, sauces, pastes & seasonings

Cafe Latte

kickstart your day

5 MIN   **SERVES 1**   **NET CARB**
0 g/serving

- 1 espresso coffee
- ½ tsp vanilla extract
- 250 ml (1 cup) almond milk, unsweetened
- 1 tbsp cream (optional)

1 Blend espresso with a hand mixer until coffee doubled in size and frothy.

2 Add vanilla extract and mix well.

3 Heat almond milk.

4 Add heated milk to coffee.

5 Pour and add cream.

6 Swizzle with a spoon to create a pattern on top and serve.

 TIP | **Almond milk offers a tasty low-carb alternative to dairy.**

Frothy Chai Latte
based on traditional chai tea

35 MIN   SERVES 2   NET CARB
0 g/serving

- ½ star anise
- 3 whole cloves
- ½ tsp vanilla extract
- 1 stick cinnamon
- pinch ground ginger
- 3 whole peppercorns
- 2 cardamom pods, opened
- 120 ml (½ cup) water
- 480 ml (2 cups) almond milk
- 2 teabags
- nutmeg, grated

1 Add spices to water in a pan.
2 Bring to boil.
3 Remove from heat and steep for 20 to 30 min depending on strength desired.
4 Add almond milk to the tea spice mixture and reheat, bringing it back to boil.
5 Remove from heat.
6 Add teabag to the mixture and allow to steep up to 5 min (depending on your taste).
7 Strain into a blender and blend for 5 seconds to make frothy.
8 Pour into 2 cups.
9 Grate nutmeg on top and serve immediately.

Turmeric Latte

so incredibly healthy

5 MIN   SERVES 1   NET CARB
                                 0 g/serving

- 250 ml (1 cup) unsweetened almond milk
- 1 tsp ground turmeric
- pinch ground ginger
- pinch pepper
- pinch ground cinnamon

1 Combine milk, turmeric, ginger and pepper in a blender.
2 Process at high speed for at least 1 min until smooth.
3 Pour into a pan and heat until just before boiling point.
4 Transfer to a mug or glass.
5 Serve with a sprinkle of cinnamon on top.

Masala Seasoning

*quick, easy-to-make, aromatic spice
mix essential for truly authentic flavour*

5 MIN   SERVES 6   NET CARB
0 g/serving

- 1 tsp ground red chilli
- 1 tsp black pepper
- 1 tsp ground coriander
- 1 tsp ground cumin
- ½ tsp ground garlic
- ½ tsp ground cardamom
- ½ tsp ground turmeric
- ½ tsp ground fennel
- ½ tsp ground cinnamon
- pinch of nutmeg

1 Add all ingredients to a bowl and mix thoroughly to make Masala seasoning.

TIP | Store in an airtight jar. Masala seasoning is used in Pav Bhaji and Tandoori Paneer Tikka recipes.

Fresh Tomato Sauce

delicious Mediterranean authentic flavour you can almost feel the sunshine!

15 MIN **SERVES 4** **NET CARB**
4 g/serving

- 4 tbsp olive oil
- 45g onion (3 tbsp), chopped
- 2 cloves garlic, chopped
- 225g (1 cup) tomatoes, finely chopped
- 1 and ½ tbsp mixed herbs
- salt and pepper

1 Fry onion for 1 min in olive oil.
2 Then add garlic and fry for a further 1 min.
3 Add tomatoes and herbs.
4 Cook for 10 min.
5 Season with salt and pepper.
6 For a smoother texture, mix for 30 seconds in a food processor.

> **TIP**
>
> Add 1 or 2 tbsp water if consistency is too sticky. Use immediately or store in fridge up to three days. Use with Papatas Bravas.

Masala Paste

spicy and wonderfully aromatic paste from Goa

10 MIN   SERVES 2   NET CARB
                                  3.5 g/serving

- 2 tsp black mustard seeds
- 1 tbsp coconut oil, melted
- 2 tsp black peppercorns
- 1 and ½ tbsp ground cumin
- 1 and ½ tbsp ground coriander
- 2 tsp garam masala
- 2 tsp ground turmeric
- ½ tsp ground cinnamon
- 1 tsp tamarind paste
- 1 tsp ground chilli
- 3 garlic cloves, chopped
- 3 cm (1 inch) piece ginger, chopped or ¼ tsp ground ginger
- splash of balsamic vinegar
- 2 tbsp olive oil

1. Fry mustard seeds in coconut oil in a pan.
2. Cook for 1 min until seeds start to 'pop'.
3. Add peppercorns, cumin, coriander, garam masala, turmeric and cinnamon.
4. Cook for 1 min.
5. Allow to cool.
6. Blend spice mix in a blender.
7. Then add tamarind paste, chilli, garlic, ginger, vinegar and olive oil.
8. Blend again until smooth.

> **TIP**
>
> Double the quantity and store it in the fridge for up to seven days. Use in Mackerel Recheado recipe.

Aioli

delicious garlicky mayonnaise

10 MIN   **SERVES 6**   **NET CARB**
1 g/serving

- 2 egg yolks
- 2 tsp Dijon mustard
- 75 ml (⅓ cup) extra virgin olive oil
- 3 garlic cloves, finely crushed
- 2 tbsp lemon juice
- salt and pepper

1 Whisk egg yolks, mustard and a pinch of salt.
2 Very, very slowly pour in olive oil, in a steady stream, whisking all the time.
3 Continue whisking until thick.
4 Add garlic, whisk again.
5 Then add lemon juice and whisk again.
6 Season to taste.
7 Can store in fridge up to five days.

> **TIP** | Serve with Waldorf Salad and Anchovy and Egg Salad with croutons. For mayonnaise, leave out the garlic.

Classic Pesto

one of our favourites and so simple to make

10 MIN   SERVES 6   NET CARB
1 g/serving

- 30g (2 tbsp) pine nuts
- ½ tbsp coconut oil
- 3 cloves garlic
- handful (½ cup) basil leaves
- 4 tbsp extra virgin olive oil
- 60g (4 tbsp) Parmesan, grated
- salt and pepper

1 Shallow fry pine nuts in coconut oil in a pan for 1 min.

2 Remove and set aside.

3 Then fry garlic cloves in pan for 1 to 2 min.

4 Add all ingredients into a processor and blend into a rough paste.

5 Transfer to a bowl.

6 Store in fridge up to five days.

Tomato and Olive Sauce

a touch of Italy, delicious with white fish

5 MIN **SERVES 2** **NET CARB**
1.5 g/serving

- 80g (⅓ cup) small black olives, pitted
- 2 tbsp olive oil
- zest of half a lemon, peeled in strips
- 1 tsp ground coriander
- 2 tsp dried sage
- 1 large ripe tomato, finely chopped
- salt and pepper

1 Heat olives in olive oil in a pan, then add lemon zest strips.
2 Add coriander, sage and tomato.
3 Cook for 5 min.
4 Season.
5 Heat through and serve over white fish.

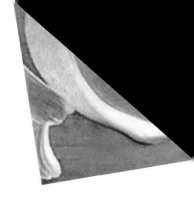

Raita

the perfect accompaniment to spicy dishes

5 MIN   SERVES 4   NET CARB
                                 2 g/serving

- 110g (½ cup) plain yoghurt
- 110g (½ cup) cucumber, chopped
- 2 tbsp fresh coriander (cilantro), chopped
- 1 salad onion, finely chopped
- ¼ tsp ground coriander
- ¼ tsp ground cumin
- 2 tsp fresh mint, chopped
- salt and pepper

1. Put the yoghurt in a bowl, and mix in all other ingredients.
2. Chill before use.
3. Store in fridge up to three days.

TIP | **Use with Spicy Mussels Rasam and Mackerel Recheado.**

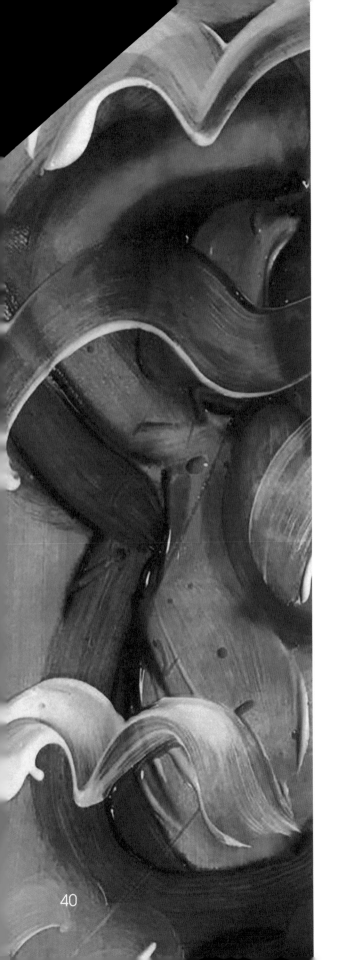

'Life without tapas
is like a heart
without love.'

B.L.S. IYENGAR

salads and light meals

Low-carb Bread

crispy on the outside, soft on the inside

60 MIN **SLICES 14** **NET CARB** 2 g/slice **175°C** (350°F)

- 300g (1¼ cups) cauliflower rice
- 3 tbsp water
- 6 large eggs, separated
- 125g (½ cup) almond flour
- 1 tbsp baking powder
- 1 tsp sea salt
- 6 tbsp melted butter
- 5 cloves garlic, finely chopped (optional, for savoury bread)
- 1 tbsp thyme
- 2 tbsp parsley, chopped
- Parmesan cheese, grated for garnish

1. Line a 9 inch x 5 inch loaf tin with baking paper.
2. Process cauliflower to rice consistency.
3. Place rice in a pan with water and cook for 3 min until soft.
4. Place cauliflower rice on a clean kitchen towel and squeeze to ensure all water is squeezed out.
5. Beat egg whites in a bowl until stiff peaks form. Set aside.
6. Mix almond flour, baking powder, salt, egg yolks, melted butter, garlic and about ¼ of the egg white mixture.
7. Beat until well mixed, then stir in cauliflower.
8. Fold in remaining egg whites and mix thoroughly until fluffy.
9. Fold in thyme and ¾ of the parsley.
10. Transfer the batter to the prepared loaf tin and sprinkle with remaining parsley.
11. Bake for 45 min until the top is golden.
12. Allow to cool before slicing.
13. Serve topped with Parmesan and parsley.

TIP | Slice and store surplus in packs of 2 or 4 slices in the freezer.

Quick Indian-style Snack

tasty and easy to make

10 MIN   **SERVES 2**   **NET CARB**
6 g/serving

- 200g cauliflower (⅔ cup)
- 2 tbsp butter/ghee
- 1 tbsp black mustard seeds
- 1 and ½ tbsp ground cumin
- 20g (1½ tbsp) onion, chopped
- 4 curry leaves
- 2 cm (⅔ inch) fresh ginger, finely chopped
- 1 green chilli, chopped
- 20g (1½ tbsp) pine nuts
- 2 tbsp yoghurt/crème fraiche
- 1 tbsp coriander (cilantro), chopped

1. Prepare cauliflower in a food processor until rice-sized.
2. Fry mustard seeds and cumin in butter.
3. When sizzling, add onion, curry leaves, ginger, chilli and nuts.
4. Lower heat and fry until onions are cooked.
5. Season with salt and pepper.
6. Add cauliflower rice, mix well and fry for a further one min.
7. Add 1 tbsp water and cook for one min.
8. Stir frequently.
9. Spoon into bowls and serve immediately.
10. Garnish with yoghurt or crème fraiche and chopped coriander.

Herby Mushrooms on Butter-Fried Bread

really quick and simply delicious for brunch or light lunch

10 MIN　　**SERVES 2**　　**NET CARB**
6 g/serving

- 30g (2 tbsp) butter
- 225g (1 cup) mushrooms, chopped
- 2 cloves garlic, chopped
- 55g (¼ cup) red pepper, chopped
- 1 tsp dried thyme
- 1 tsp dried parsley
- 2 slices low-carb bread (see p43)
- 2 tbsp crème fraiche
- 2 tsp chives, chopped

1. Melt 1 tbsp butter in a frying pan.
2. Fry low-carb bread in butter until crispy.
3. Set aside.
4. Using the same pan, add 1 tbsp butter then mushrooms, garlic and red pepper.
5. Fry for 2 or 3 min.
6. Add thyme and parsley for a further 30 seconds.
7. Season with salt and pepper.
8. Serve immediately on fried low-carb bread.
9. Spoon crème fraiche over mushrooms.
10. Garnish with chives.

Smoked Salmon with Creamy Horseradish

appetising and nutritious quick snack

5 MIN   SERVES 2   NET CARB
                                 3 g/serving

- 200g (7 oz) smoked salmon, sliced
- 1 tsp creamed horseradish
- 3 tbsp crème fraiche
- zest of half a lemon
- fennel leaves, for garnish
- salt and black pepper
- 1 lemon, quartered
- 2 slices low-carb bread (see p43)

1 Arrange salmon slices on a plate.
2 Mix horseradish, crème fraiche, lemon zest and salt in a bowl.
3 Spoon delicately over salmon.
4 Grind black pepper over sauce and salmon.
5 Decorate with fennel leaves on the side.
6 Serve with lemon quarters and low-carb bread.

Waldorf Salad

crunchy tempting salad

15 MIN   SERVES 2   NET CARB
                                  14 g/serving

- 2 celery stalks, chopped
- 75g (⅓ cup) strawberries, sliced
- 170g (¾ cup) feta cheese, crumbled
- 80g (⅓ cup) walnuts, chopped
- lettuce, shredded

Dressing
- 4 tbsp cream cheese
- 6 tbsp homemade Aioli (see p33)
- 3 tbsp lemon juice
- salt

1 Make dressing whisking cream cheese, mayonnaise (Aioli) and lemon juice until smooth.

2 Stir celery, strawberries, feta and walnuts into a bowl.

3 Add dressing and mix thoroughly.

4 Serve immediately on a bed of lettuce.

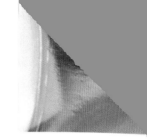

Avocado Salad

a deliciously appealing quick dish

10 MIN　　**SERVES 2**　　**NET CARB**
9 g/serving

- 110g (½ cup) halloumi, diced
- 2 tbsp olive oil
- 2 avocados, sliced
- 2 medium tomatoes, sliced
- 55g (¼ cup) cucumber, diced
- 2 tbsp pine nuts
- 2 salad onions, finely chopped
- 55g radishes (¼ cup), chopped
- 1 jalapeño, chopped
- 2 tsp mixed herbs
- 2 tbsp olive oil
- 1 lime, juiced

1 Fry halloumi in olive oil for a few min until golden.

2 Make salad in a bowl, adding avocado, tomatoes, cucumber, pine nuts, salad onions and radishes topped with jalapeño and herbs.

3 Dress with olive oil and lime juice.

4 Toss halloumi on top and serve immediately.

TIP | **Instead of halloumi, substitute 150g (⅔ cup) smoked mackerel or 150g (⅔ cup) cooked salmon as alternative protein sources.**

Marinated Olives

great for extra flavour

5 MIN   SERVES 6   NET CARB
                                 1 g/serving

- 1 lime/lemon, peeled for zest
- 1 tbsp parsley, chopped
- 2 tsp fresh rosemary, chopped
- 2 tsp fresh thyme, chopped,
- 1 clove garlic, chopped
- 2 bay leaves
- ½ red chilli, chopped (optional)
- 3 tbsp olive oil
- 170g (¾ cup) olives
- salt and pepper

1 Using a potato peeler, cut the lime/lemon skin into strips.

2 Mix the strips with parsley, rosemary, thyme, garlic, bay leaf and chilli with olive oil; season with salt and pepper.

3 Add olives and marinate overnight.

4 Store in fridge.

> **TIP** | For variation, add 110g (½ cup) of cubed feta cheese into the olive mixture.

Tapas: Patatas Bravas
surprise yourself, tantalising tapas!

10 MIN **SERVES 4** **NET CARB**
3 g/serving

- 350g (1½ cups) radishes
- 1½ tbsp olive oil
- ¼ tsp dried chilli flakes
- 1½ tsp Tabasco sauce
- 1½ tsp red wine vinegar
- 60 ml (4 tbsp) tomato sauce (see p29)
- ½ tsp smoked paprika
- salt and pepper

1 Heat olive oil in a pan, add radishes and stir to coat with olive oil.
2 Add 1 or 2 tbsp water and steam (with the lid on) for 2 min.
3 Add more oil to the pan, then add chilli, Tabasco, and red wine vinegar.
4 Mix well and fry on medium to high heat for 3 or 4 min to roast radishes on both sides.
5 Stir in tomato sauce.
6 Season with salt and pepper.
7 Plate radishes and tomato sauce and sprinkle with paprika.

Fish Tapas

an inviting healthy snack

10 MIN **SERVES 4** **NET CARB**
5 g/serving

- 75g (⅓ cup) firm white fish, cubed
- 75g (⅓ cup) prawns (shrimp)
- 75g (⅓ cup) red mullet, cubed
- 75g squid (⅓ cup), tentacles and all, cut in rings
- 3 tbsp almond flour, for coating fish
- 90 ml (8 tbsp) olive oil
- 1 lemon, cut in wedges
- salt and pepper

1 Toss fish with flour in a bowl, ensuring fish is completely covered.
2 Heat olive oil and fry fish in a pan for a few mins.
3 Plate fish, season with salt and pepper.
4 Serve with lemon wedges.

TIP | **Serve with Patatas Bravas.**

Goat's Cheese on Low-carb Bread

an appetising quick snack

10 MIN   **SERVES 2**   **NET CARB**
4 g/serving

GRILL

- 2 slices low-carb bread (see p43)
- 2 tbsp olive oil
- 30g (2 tbsp) pesto (see p35)
- 2 slices goat's cheese
- mixed salad leaves with baby
- tomatoes
- 2 tbsp walnut oil

1 Using a frying pan, add olive oil and fry bread for one min each side until crispy.

2 Spread 1 tbsp pesto on each slice before adding the cheese slice.

3 Plate the bread under a hot grill and quickly grill the bread and cheese until cheese is bubbling.

4 Prepare salad leaves and toss the leaves and tomatoes in walnut oil.

5 Plate the salad and top with crispy cheese bread slices.

Asparagus with Salsa Verde

tangy zesty flavour

10 MIN   SERVES 2   NET CARB
1.5 g/serving

- 10 asparagus spears, trimmed
- 4 tbsp olive oil
- 1 tbsp fresh parsley, chopped
- 2 tbsp fresh basil, chopped
- 1 clove garlic, chopped
- 1 tbsp mint, chopped
- 1 tbsp capers (optional)
- 1 tsp Dijon mustard
- zest of half a lemon, grated
- salt and pepper
- 1 tsp parsley, chopped
- 1 anchovy (optional)

1. Wash asparagus and fry in 1 tbsp olive oil.
2. Season with salt and pepper.
3. Add 1 tbsp water and steam for a further 1 min.
4. Process parsley, basil, garlic, mint, capers, mustard, lemon zest and remaining olive oil.
5. Transfer to a bowl and season to taste.
6. Serve over asparagus spears.
7. Garnish with parsley and anchovy (if using).

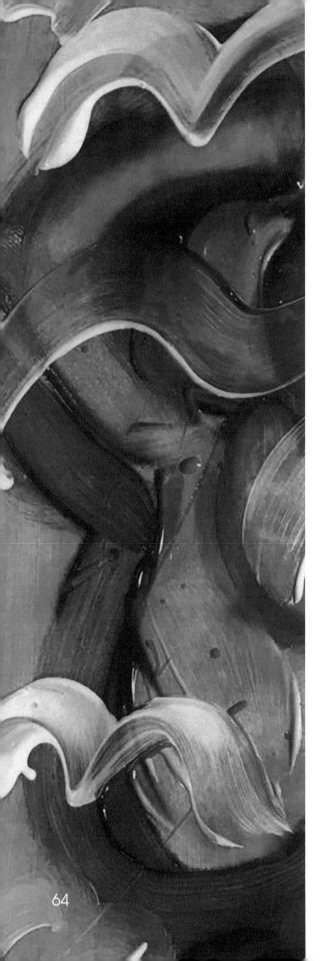

'Vegetables, herbs and spices. If you can combine these ingredients, that should be the best dish you would ever cook!'

RINRIN MARINKA

vegetables mains and sides

Vegetable Rice

a grain-free, great low-carb replacement for rice

20 MIN   SERVES 2   NET CARB
4 g/serving

- 225g (1 cup) cauliflower); or 225g (1 cup) broccoli); or 225g (1 cup) courgettes (zucchini), cut in florets or chunks
- 2 tbsp olive oil
- 2 tbsp butter
- salt and pepper

1 Place vegetables of your choice in a food processor, pulse on and off quickly until it forms 'rough grains'.

2 Don't overdo it – it is essential to preserve the texture of the vegetables and not let them go to mush.

3 Drizzle olive oil into a large frying pan, add salt and pepper and spread the oil around the base to prevent vegetables from sticking.

4 Turn the heat up high.

5 Add vegetables and stir briskly for 2 or 3 min.

6 Add butter, allowing it to melt.

7 Serve immediately.

Zoodles

a healthy low-carb alternative to spaghetti

5 MIN   SERVES 2   NET CARB
                                 5 g/serving

- 225g (1 cup) courgettes (zucchini) or 225g (1 cup) cabbage
- 1 tbsp olive oil
- 2 cloves garlic, chopped
- 2 tbsp mascarpone
- salt and pepper
- 2 tbsp Parmesan cheese, grated

1 Spiralise the vegetables.
2 Fry garlic in olive oil for 1 min.
3 Add salt and pepper.
4 Add spiralised vegetables for 1 min (less if you like your vegetables al dente).
5 Add mascarpone.
6 Sprinkle with Parmesan and serve immediately.

Creamy Cauliflower Mash

a delicious low carb alternative to mashed potatoes

10 MIN   **SERVES 2**   **NET CARB**
5 g/serving

- 225g (1 cup) cauliflower, florets
- 2 cloves garlic, chopped
- 1 tsp thyme
- 75g (5 tbsp) butter
- 2 tbsp water
- 2 tbsp cream
- salt and pepper

1. Fry garlic in butter for 1 min.
2. Add thyme.
3. Add cauliflower florets and stir, coating the florets with butter.
4. Add water and steam for 2 to 3 min.
5. Mash well.
6. Season with salt and pepper.
7. Add cream and serve immediately.

Cabbage Stir Fry

use this delicious healthy alternative for pasta

10 MIN   **SERVES 2**   **NET CARB**
7 g/serving

- 110g (½ cup) cauliflower, chopped into small pieces
- 150g (⅔ cup) cabbage, shredded
- 4 tbsp butter
- ½ tsp each ground chilli, ground coriander, ground cinnamon and turmeric
- 2 tsp white wine vinegar
- 2 tsp thyme
- 20g (1½ tbsp) onion, sliced
- 1 clove garlic, chopped
- handful parsley, chopped
- 2 tbsp mascarpone
- salt and pepper

1 Fry all spices, wine vinegar and thyme in butter for 30 seconds.
2 Add cauliflower, cabbage and onion.
3 Fry for 2 min coating the vegetables with all the spice mix.
4 Add garlic and lightly fry for further 30 seconds.
5 Season with salt and pepper.
6 Garnish with parsley and serve immediately with mascarpone.

Middle Eastern Butter Bean Stew

packed with flavour

| 45 MIN | SERVES 2 | NET CARB 16 g/serving | 175°C (350°F) | |

- 20g (1½ tbsp) onion, chopped
- 300g (1⅓ cup) peppers, red and/or yellow, chopped
- 2 cloves garlic, chopped
- 2 tbsp thyme, chopped
- 4 tbsp olive oil
- 110g (½ cup) butter beans (canned)
- 1 tsp allspice
- 150g (⅔ cup) green beans, topped and tailed
- 2 tbsp natural (plain) yoghurt

1 Add onion, peppers and garlic to a roasting tin.
2 Sprinkle thyme over vegetables.
3 Cover with 3 tbsp olive oil.
4 Bake for 20 min.
5 Add butter beans and allspice, mix well.
6 Add more olive oil if necessary.
7 Bake for a further 20 min.
8 Using a fresh pan, quick fry green beans for 1 min in 1 tbsp olive oil.
9 Season with salt and pepper.
10 Add 1 tbsp water, close lid and steam for 2 min.
11 Mix beans with roast vegetables.
12 Serve immediately with yoghurt on the side.

> ALERT | Butter beans have a high net carb value.

Pav Bhaji

spicy Indian vegetable dish

15 MIN **SERVES 2** **NET CARB**
11.5 g/serving

- 300g (1⅛ cup) cauliflower, chopped
- 2 tbsp coconut oil
- 110g (½ cup) tomatoes, chopped
- ½ red or yellow pepper, chopped
- 1 cm (⅜ inch) fresh ginger, chopped
- 1 tsp masala seasoning (see p27)
- 3 tbsp butter
- 15g (1 tbsp) onion, sliced
- 1 tsp parsley, chopped
- ½ tsp ground chilli
- ½ tsp fenugreek seeds
- ½ lime, juiced
- salt
- 2 slices low-carb bread (see p43)

1 Fry cauliflower in coconut oil for 1 min.
2 Add tomatoes, pepper, ginger, a pinch of the masala seasoning, salt and ½ the butter.
3 Mix well and cook for 2 min.
4 Mash the mixture to a rough paste and transfer to a bowl.
5 Set aside.
6 Heat remaining butter in the same pan and add onion, parsley, fenugreek, chilli and the remaining masala seasoning.
7 Cook for 2 or 3 min.
8 Add cauliflower mash, mix well and cook for a further 2 min.
9 Depending on how soft you want your mixture to be, you can mash it again (adding 1 tbsp water if required).
10 Add lime juice and season with salt.
11 Serve with a slice of low-carb bread.

Nut Roast

a traditional vegetarian dish

70 MIN **SERVES 3-4** **NET CARB** 7 g/serving **175°C** (350°F)

- 1 tbsp olive oil
- 55g (¼ cup) spinach
- 110g (½ cup) mixed nuts (almonds, brazil nuts, hazelnuts and pecans)
- 20g sundried tomatoes, chopped
- 55g (¼ cup) carrot, grated
- 1 egg, whisked
- 55g (¼ cup) strong Cheddar, grated
- pinch of dried sage
- 1 tsp fresh parsley
- 1 clove garlic, chopped
- 1 tsp pesto
- 1 tsp basil, chopped
- 225g (1 cup) green vegetables
- salt and pepper

1. Grease a baking tin with olive oil.
2. Add spinach to a food processor.
3. Pulse processor, then add nuts until finely chopped.
4. Do not over process, as it will turn to flour.
5. Add sundried tomatoes to the blend.
6. Pour the processed mixture into a bowl, add all other ingredients and thoroughly mix.
7. Add the mixture to the baking tin, making sure the top is smooth.
8. Cover with greaseproof paper so the top does not burn.
9. Bake for 45 min.
10. Serve with green vegetables.

Indian Roasted Cauliflower

side dish, spicy and flavoursome

20 MIN **SERVES 2** **NET CARB** 3.5 g/serving **200°C** (400°F)

- 2 tbsp butter/ghee
- 30g (2 tbsp) pine nuts
- 150g (⅔ cup) cauliflower, cut in florets

Spice mix
- 1 tsp each ground cumin, ground coriander, turmeric; ½ tsp ground chilli, salt and pepper
- 1 tsp lemon juice

Yoghurt dressing
- 2 tbsp natural (plain) yoghurt
- 1 tsp mint, chopped
- handful coriander (cilantro), chopped

1 Fry spice mix and nuts in butter for 2 min.
2 Add cauliflower and toss florets in the spice mix.
3 Cook for 2 or 3 min.
4 Toss lemon juice over.
5 Place in ovenproof dish and roast for 10 to 15 min.
6 Combine yoghurt and mint.
7 Served topped with coriander and minty yoghurt sauce.

Roasted Peppers with Baby Tomatoes

zingy flavours

| 30 MIN | SERVES 2 | NET CARB 8 g/serving | 200°C (400°F) |

- 300g (1¼ cup), 2 red peppers
- 2 tbsp olive oil
- 10 baby tomatoes, halved
- handful basil leaves, chopped
- 2 cloves garlic, chopped
- 2 tbsp pesto
- salt and pepper

1 Oil an ovenproof dish, halve red peppers lengthwise removing seeds, arrange peppers in the dish.

2 Toss tomatoes in a bowl with basil and garlic.

3 Add remaining olive oil and season with salt and pepper.

4 Divide mixture for the peppers.

5 Top each pepper with pesto.

6 Roast in the oven for 20 min.

7 Serve as a side dish.

'The egg is
a symbol of
perfection.'

MASON COOLEY

eggs

French Toast

great for breakfast, lunch or dinner

15 MIN   **SERVES 2**   **NET CARB**
9.5 g/serving

- 1 egg
- 40ml milk
- 20ml cream
- ½ tsp vanilla extract
- ¼ tsp ground cinnamon
- 4 slices homemade low-carb bread (see recipe p43)
- 3 tbsp butter
- 100g fresh berries
- 2 tbsp mascarpone

1 Whisk egg, milk, cream, vanilla and cinnamon together.
2 Place slices of bread in a shallow dish and pour the egg mixture over.
3 Soak for 3 mins, then turn over and soak the other side for 2 mins.
4 Heat butter in a frying pan.
5 Fry the soaked bread for 3 mins on each side until golden and crispy.
6 Serve with berries on top and mascarpone on the side.

Tunisian Chakchouka

fiery and garlicky

40 MIN   SERVES 2   NET CARB 11 g/serving   200°C (400°F)

- 225g (1 cup) red/yellow peppers, sliced
- 15g (1 tbsp) red onion, sliced
- 110g (½ cup) aubergine (eggplant), sliced
- 170g (¾ cup) tomatoes, halved
- 2 cloves garlic, chopped
- ½ chilli, finely chopped
- 1 and ½ tsp Harissa paste
- 3 tbsp olive oil
- 1 tsp ground cumin
- 4 eggs
- salt and pepper

1. Place peppers, onion, aubergine, tomatoes, garlic and chilli in a roasting tray.
2. Mix harissa paste with olive oil and cover vegetables.
3. Sprinkle cumin on top.
4. Season with salt and pepper.
5. Roast at 200°C (400°F) for 20 min.
6. Remove tray from oven.
7. Make 4 indentations in the vegetable mixture.
8. Crack one egg into each and season with salt and pepper.
9. Reduce oven temp to 180°C (360°F) and bake for further 12 min.

Classic Pissaladière

France's answer to pizza, a great summer dish

35 MIN   SERVES 2   NET CARB   200°C
                                  7 g/serving   (400 F)

Pastry crust
- 2 eggs
- 110g (½ cup) mozzarella
- 1 tbsp butter

Topping
- 15g (1 tbsp) shallot, chopped
- 1 clove garlic, chopped
- 55g (¼ cup) courgette (zucchini), chopped
- 110g (½ cup) tomatoes, sliced
- 55g (¼ cup) tinned artichoke hearts, quartered
- handful fresh herbs: basil, rosemary, thyme, sage; chopped
- 6 anchovy fillets
- 75g (⅓ cup) Parmesan, grated
- 2 tbsp olive oil
- salt and pepper
- mixed green salad leaves
- 2 tbsp walnut oil

1. To make the crust, mix eggs and mozzarella.
2. Spread butter on baking paper on a baking tray (use silicone mat if preferred).
3. Form the egg and mozzarella mixture into a rectangular shape on the buttered paper.
4. Bake for 15 min.
5. Remove from oven and scatter shallots, garlic and courgette over the pastry base.
6. Arrange tomato slices from the dough rim inwards.
7. Fill any gaps with artichoke hearts.
8. Season with herbs and salt and pepper.
9. Sprinkle with Parmesan and olive oil.
10. Bake for a further 10 to 15 min.
11. Serve with a mixed green salad dressed with walnut oil.

Indian Frittata
with a spicy twist

25 MIN

SERVES 2

NET CARB
6 g/serving

200°C
(400°F)

- 15g (1 tbsp) shallots, sliced
- 2 cloves garlic, chopped
- 2 tbsp butter/ghee
- 150g (⅔ cup) cauliflower, finely chopped
- 3 eggs
- 2 tbsp milk
- 1 tsp garam masala
- ½ tsp turmeric

Yoghurt dressing
- 1 clove garlic, minced,
- 2 tsp lemon juice,
- 1 tsp white wine vinegar,
- 1 tbsp plain yoghurt,
- 1 tbsp olive oil
- salt and pepper

1. Fry shallot and garlic in 1 tbsp butter in a frying pan.
2. Quickly add cauliflower and stir into the onion/garlic mixture.
3. Add 1 tbsp water.
4. Steam for 1 min.
5. Whisk eggs and milk, adding garam masala, turmeric, salt and pepper.
6. Pour egg mixture into pan over vegetables and stir thoroughly.
7. Grease ovenproof dish with butter and transfer egg mixture and bake for 20 min.
8. Make yoghurt dressing by combining all dressing ingredients, adding olive oil last.
9. Season with salt and pepper.
10. Serve immediately.

Quick Eggs Traybake

easy-peasy

15 MIN   **SERVES 2**   **NET CARB** 4 g/serving   **165°C** (325°F)

- 4 free-range eggs
- 150g (⅔ cup) red pepper, sliced
- 110g (½ cup) mushrooms, sliced
- 75g (⅓ cup) spinach
- 75g (⅓ cup) strong cheddar, grated
- salt and pepper

1 Grease ovenproof dish.
2 Whisk eggs in a bowl and season.
3 Pour egg mixture into dish.
4 Scatter pepper, mushrooms and spinach over egg mixture.
5 Top with cheddar.
6 Bake for 10 to 15 min.
7 Cut into slices and serve.

> **TIP** | Can keep in the fridge in a sealed container for up to 3 days and can be eaten cold.

Anchovy and Egg Salad with Croutons

served with garlic mayonnaise, a quick, easy lunch

20 MIN **SERVES 2** **NET CARB 6 g/serving**

- 2 eggs, boiled
- 1 gem lettuce
- 1 large tomato, sliced
- 20g black olives
- 1 small tin anchovy fillets
- 2 tbsp Aioli (p33)
- 2 slices low-carb bread for croutons (see p43)
- 2 tbsp coconut oil
- 1 tbsp parsley, chopped

1 Boil 2 eggs and cut them in half.
2 Arrange lettuce leaves on a plate, add tomato, black olives and eggs.
3 Cover with individual anchovy fillets.
4 Add 1 tbsp Aioli to each plate.
5 Add coconut oil to a frying pan, heat oil and add croutons.
6 Fry for 2 or 3 min.
7 Garnish salad with croutons and top with parsley.

Smoked Salmon and Creamy Egg Pots

healthy super quick snack

15 MIN   **SERVES 2**   **NET CARB**   200°C
                                         3.5 g/serving   (400 F)

- 1 tbsp butter
- 2 slices smoked salmon, cut into slivers
- 2 eggs
- 3 tbsp mascarpone
- 1 tbsp cream
- zest of half a lemon
- salt and pepper
- 15g (1 tbsp) parsley, chopped
- 2 slices low-carb bread (see p43)
- 1 tbsp butter

1 Butter two ramekins and line with smoked salmon.
2 Break an egg into the middle of each ramekin.
3 Whisk mascarpone, cream and lemon zest.
4 Pour half over each egg and season with salt and pepper.
5 Top with parsley.
6 Place ramekins in an ovenproof dish with 1cm water in the dish to act as a bain-marie.
7 Bake in the oven for 12 or 15 min until just set.
8 Serve immediately with a slice of buttered low-carb bread.

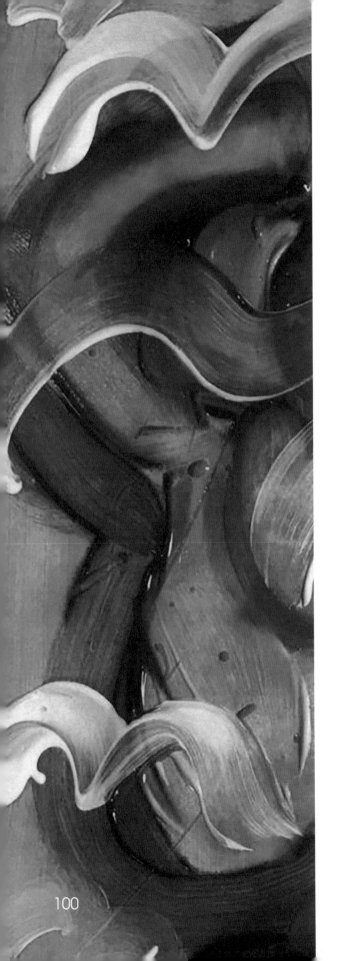

'It is health that is
real wealth and
not pieces of gold
and silver.'

MAHATMA GANDHI

vegetables with cheese

Spicy Eastern Mediterranean Vegetable Bake

very traditional dish

65 MIN   **SERVES 2**   **NET CARB**
20 g/serving   **200°C**
(400°F)

- 400g (1½ cups) medium courgettes (zucchini), sliced in half
- 120g (½ a drained can) chickpeas (garbanzo beans)
- 5 tbsp olive oil
- 2 cloves garlic, chopped
- 150g (⅔ cup) green beans, topped and tailed
- 110g (½ cup) feta cheese, crumbled
- 2 medium tomatoes, sliced
- 2 tsp thyme, chopped
- 1 red chilli, finely chopped
- 2 tbsp parsley, chopped

1 Place courgettes in an ovenproof dish with chickpeas, garlic and salt.
2 Drizzle with 3 tbsp olive oil.
3 Roast for 20 min at 200°C (400°F).
4 Add green beans coated with 2 tbsp olive oil.
5 Place feta over vegetables.
6 Add sliced tomatoes.
7 Add salt and pepper and half chilli, and sprinkle thyme over the entire dish.
8 Turn oven down to 180°C (350°F) for a further 30 min.
9 Garnish with remaining chilli and parsley.
10 Serve immediately.

TIP Using 4 poached eggs as an alternative to chickpeas will reduce the net carb value per serving to 15g.

Creamy Radish Gnocchi with Olives and Gorgonzola

use low-carb radishes instead of potatoes

10 MIN   **SERVES 2**   **NET CARB** 6.5 g/serving

- 4 tbsp olive oil
- 150g (⅔ cup) radishes, halved
- 15g (1 tbsp) shallot, sliced
- 2 cloves garlic, chopped
- 55g (¼ cup) olives (green or black), pitted
- 90ml (6 tbsp) cream
- 110g (½ cup) Gorgonzola, crumbled
- 10 anchovy fillets, drained and washed (optional)
- 2 salad onions, chopped
- 170g (¾ cup) spinach (see tip on right)

1 Fry radishes and shallot in olive oil for 2 min then add garlic for a further 1 min.

2 Stir in olives.

3 Add cream and heat through.

4 Add Gorgonzola and anchovies and cook until cheese has melted.

5 Garnish with chopped onions and spinach on the side.

6 Serve immediately.

TIP Use wilted spinach as an accompaniment. Fry spinach in olive oil, season with salt and pepper, add 1 tbsp water and steam for 2 min. Serve immediately with gnocchi.

Aubergine Parmigiana

classic bake dish, brilliant nutritious low-carb alternative to lasagna

45 MIN   **SERVES 2**   **NET CARB** 17 g/serving   175°C (350°F)

- 3 tbsp olive oil
- 15g (1 tbsp) onion, sliced
- 2 garlic cloves, chopped
- 170g (¾ cup) tomatoes, chopped
- 2 tbsp parsley, chopped
- 2 tsp dried basil
- 2 tsp dried thyme
- 300g (1⅓ cup) aubergine (eggplant)
- 110g (1 cup) mozzarella, shredded
- 55g (¼ cup) Parmesan
- 225 ml (1 cup) cream
- salt and pepper
- 1 gem lettuce
- 100g tomatoes, sliced
- basil leaves for garnish

1 Fry onion and garlic in 1 tbsp olive oil.

2 Add tomatoes, parsley, basil and thyme.

3 Season and simmer for 20 min.

4 Slice aubergines in thin slices and brush with remaining olive oil.

5 Season.

6 Fry aubergines for 2 min each side.

7 Using an ovenproof dish, place one layer of tomato mixture followed by a layer of aubergines; continue alternating tomato mixture and aubergines finishing with tomato mixture on top.

8 Place mozzarella on top and cover with Parmesan.

9 Bake in the oven for 20 min.

10 Add cream for the last 5 min in the oven.

11 Garnish with basil leaves and serve with lettuce and tomato salad.

Faux Pasta with Brussels Sprouts topped with Cheese

clever use of shredded cabbage as pasta

25 MIN   SERVES 2   NET CARB 10 g/serving   200°C (400°F)

- 150g (⅔ cup) Brussels sprouts, halved
- 150g (⅔ cup) cabbage, shredded
- 30g (2 tbsp) butter
- 110g (½ cup) ricotta
- 110g (½ cup) Gruyère, grated
- 30g (2 tbsp) butter
- 1 tsp sage
- 2 cloves garlic, chopped
- 55g (¼ cup) Parmesan, grated

1. Fry sprouts and cabbage in butter for 2 min, add salt and pepper.
2. Add 2 tbsp water to pan and steam for 2 or 3 mins.
3. Mix ricotta into vegetables.
4. Add vegetable mixture to an ovenproof dish and cover with Gruyère.
5. Add 1 or 2 tbsp water if required.
6. Fry garlic in butter and add sage for the final 30 seconds.
7. Pour over pasta bake.
8. Top with Parmesan.
9. Bake for 15 to 20 min.

Stuffed Peppers

loaded with flavour

30 MIN   SERVES 2   NET CARB 12 g/serving   200°C (400°F)

- 225g (1 cup) cauliflower rice (see p67)
- 2 red/yellow medium peppers
- 2 tbsp olive oil
- 15g (1 tbsp) shallot, thinly sliced
- 110g (½ cup) courgette (zucchini), chopped
- 75g (⅓ cup) cherry tomatoes, chopped
- 2 garlic cloves, chopped
- 1 tsp ground cumin
- 1 tsp ground coriander
- 15g (1 tbsp) toasted flaked almonds or pine nuts
- ½ orange, zest finely grated
- 3 tbsp coriander (cilantro), chopped
- 110g (½ cup) goat's cheese
- salt and pepper

1 Prepare cauliflower rice and set aside.

2 Halve peppers horizontally, discarding the seeds.

3 Place halved peppers (open side up) on baking tray pre-greased with 1 tbsp olive oil.

4 Bake for 15 min.

5 Fry shallot and courgette in 1 tbsp olive oil for 2 min.

6 Add tomatoes, garlic, cumin and coriander and cook for 1 min.

7 Tip tomato mixture into a bowl and stir in nuts and orange zest.

8 Add cauliflower rice and chopped coriander and season with salt and pepper.

9 Fill pepper halves with rice mixture, top with cheese and place back in the oven for 10 min.

10 Serve immediately.

Neapolitan Bake

packed with goodness

55 MIN   SERVES 2   NET CARB
9 g/serving   200°C
(400°F)

- 2 tbsp olive oil
- 15g (1 tbsp) shallot, chopped
- 2 cloves garlic, chopped
- 2 tsp tomato puree
- 110g (1 cup) tomatoes, chopped
- 45 ml (3 tbsp) vegetable stock
- 1 tsp Worcester sauce
- 1 tbsp butter
- 110g (½ cup) mushrooms, chopped
- 1 tbsp thyme
- 110g (½ cup) cabbage, finely sliced
- 1 tbsp olive oil
- 110g (½ cup) pecorino, grated
- 15g (1 tbsp) Parmesan, grated
- salt and black pepper

1 Fry shallot and garlic in olive oil.

2 Add tomato puree, tomatoes, stock, and Worcester sauce.

3 Add 1 tbsp butter to a separate pan, fry mushrooms and thyme, then add to the Neapolitan tomato mixture.

4 Cook for 10 min.

5 Prepare cabbage.

6 Fry in olive oil, seasoning with salt and pepper.

7 Add 1 tbsp water and steam for 2 or 3 min.

8 Add cabbage to Neapolitan tomato mixture and spoon into an ovenproof dish.

9 Cover with cheeses and bake for 20 min in the oven.

10 Serve with gem lettuce and tomato salad topped with chopped basil leaves.

Paneer Keema

a simple everyday Indian dish

10 MIN **SERVES 2** **NET CARB**
8 g/serving

- 15g (1 tbsp) onion, chopped
- 2 cloves garlic, chopped
- 1 tsp ground cumin
- 2 tbsp butter/ghee
- 225g (1 cup) paneer, diced
- 55g (¼ cup) tomato, chopped
- 1 cm (½ inch) fresh ginger, chopped
- ½ tsp each turmeric, ground chilli, ground coriander and garam masala
- 60 ml (4 tbsp) cream
- handful fresh coriander (cilantro), chopped
- 225g (1 cup) spinach, wilted
- salt

1 Fry onions and garlic and cumin in butter.
2 Add paneer and continue frying.
3 Add tomatoes, ginger, salt, turmeric, chilli, coriander and garam masala and mix well.
4 Keep stirring, add cream.
5 Serve immediately.
6 Garnish with coriander.
7 Serve with wilted spinach on the side.

TIP Use wilted spinach as an accompaniment. Fry spinach in olive oil, season with salt and pepper. Add 1 tbsp water and steam for 2 min.

Tandoori Paneer Tikka

marinade is key to flavour

2 H 10MIN   **SERVES 2**   **NET CARB**
7 g/serving

Marinade

- 1 tbsp butter/ghee
- 1 cm (½ inch) ginger, chopped
- 1 clove garlic, chopped
- 1 tbsp yoghurt or cream
- 1 tbsp lime juice
- 2 tsp masala seasoning (see p27)
- salt

Main dish

- 15g (1 tbsp) onion, sliced
- 55g (¼ cup) green pepper, sliced
- 110g (½ cup) paneer, cubed
- 2 tbsp coconut oil
- 1 lime, juiced

1 Mix butter, ginger, garlic and yoghurt or cream.

2 Add lime juice, masala seasoning and salt.

3 Stir well to combine.

4 Slice onion and green pepper and cut paneer into individual cubes.

5 Marinate the paneer and the vegetables for a few hours at least.

6 Fry all ingredients in a pan with coconut oil until vegetables are charred and the paneer has turned golden.

7 Drizzle with lime juice for extra flavour.

Roasted Radishes

side dish

| 55 MIN | SERVES 2 | NET CARB
2 g/serving | 200°C
(400°F) |

- 110g (½ cup) radishes, halved
- 2 cloves garlic, chopped
- 2 tbsp olive oil
- 1 tsp thyme
- 55g (¼ cup) Gruyère, grated

1 Brush olive oil on a baking dish.

2 Add radishes and garlic to an ovenproof dish.

3 Drizzle with olive oil, add thyme and season with salt and pepper.

4 Roast for 35 min until crisp.

5 Sprinkle with Gruyère and bake for a further 5 min.

6 Serve immediately.

TIP

Radishes are an excellent alternative to potatoes, having far fewer carbs. Potatoes (100g) have 15g net carbs, whereas 100g radishes have only 3g!

One-Pan Indian Cuisine

a quick and easy dish

10 MIN **SERVES 2** **NET CARB**
9 g/serving

Seasoning
- 1 tsp each salt, ginger, garam masala
- ½ tsp each turmeric and cumin
- 1 clove garlic, minced

Main dish
- 225g (1 cup) paneer, diced
- 1 tbsp ghee/butter
- 15g (1 tbsp) onion, chopped
- ½ red bell pepper, diced
- 225 (1 cup) cauliflower rice (see p67)
- salt and pepper
- 2 tsp lemon juice
- small handful coriander (cilantro), chopped

1. Make seasoning mix in a small bowl.
2. Toss paneer into the bowl and cover with seasoning.
3. Make cauliflower rice.
4. Fry paneer, onion, red pepper in butter until the paneer is golden.
5. Add cauliflower rice and lemon juice and season with salt and pepper.
6. Add 2 or 3 tbsp water to moisten if required.
7. Serve immediately topped with chopped coriander.

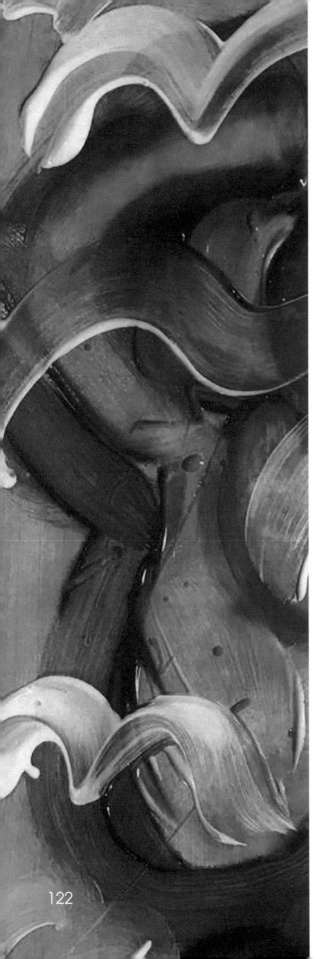

'You don't have
to cook fancy
or complicated
masterpieces. Just
good food from
fresh ingredients.'

JULIA CHILD

seafood

Paella

a low-carb spin on a classic Spanish dish

15 MIN   **SERVES 2**   **NET CARB**
10 g/serving

- 225g (1 cup) cauliflower rice
- (see p67)
- 3 tbsp olive oil
- 55g (¼ cup) tomato, chopped
- 75g (⅓ cup) red/yellow peppers, chopped
- 55g (¼ cup) green beans, chopped
- 15g (1 tbsp) onion, chopped
- 2 garlic cloves, chopped
- 1 tsp smoked paprika
- few strands saffron
- 110g (1 cup) prawns (shrimp)
- 110g (1 cup) calamari (squid), sliced
- handful of mussels
- handful parsley
- ½ lemon, halved

1 Prepare cauliflower rice and set aside.
2 Add 2 tbsp olive oil to a large frying pan.
3 Fry tomato, peppers, green beans, onion and garlic for 2 to 3 min.
4 Add paprika and salt and pepper.
5 Mix saffron in a few tbsp water and add to the pan.
6 Add prawns, calamari and mussels.
7 Cook for several min, mixing thoroughly together.
8 Add the cauliflower rice and cook through for 2 min.
9 Serve garnished with parsley and lemon quarters.

Creamy Crab Omelette

quick and easy

10 MIN   **SERVES 2**   **NET CARB**
3 g/serving

- 1 tbsp butter
- 15g (1 tbsp) shallot, chopped
- 1 clove garlic, chopped
- 4 eggs
- 1 tbsp mascarpone
- 55g (¼ cup) extra mature Gouda, grated
- 110g (½ cup) white crab meat
- 55g (¼ cup) brown crab meat
- 2 tbsp chopped herbs (parsley, chives and tarragon)
- salt and pepper

Mozzarella salad
- 1 gem lettuce, shredded
- 75g mozzarella ball, shredded
- 6 cherry tomatoes, halved
- 4 tbsp olive oil
- 2 tbsp balsamic vinegar

1 Prepare mozzarella salad, dress with olive oil and balsamic vinegar.
2 Fry shallot and garlic in butter.
3 Whisk eggs in a bowl and mix in mascarpone.
4 Add egg mixture to the frying pan.
5 Immediately stir in cheese, crab meat and herbs.
6 Reduce heat and turn one side of the omelette over the other to form a semi-circle.
7 Cut in two and serve immediately.
8 Serve with mozzarella dressed with oil and vinegar.

Creamy Salmon Pasta Bake

quick and easy

25 MIN   SERVES 2   NET CARB
7 g/serving   200°C
(400°F)

- 150g (⅔ cup) cabbage, shredded, or 150g (⅔ cup) broccoli, florets
- 2 tbsp olive oil
- 1 can Pacific salmon
- a handful of basil leaves, chopped
- 110g (½ cup) cherry tomatoes, chopped
- 2 tbsp mascarpone
- 75g (⅓ cup) mozzarella, grated
- 15g (1tbsp) pine nuts
- 1 tbsp butter
- mixed lettuce leaf salad
- 1 tbsp olive oil
- 1 tbsp balsamic vinegar
- salt and pepper

1. Fry vegetables in olive oil.
2. Season with salt and pepper.
3. Add 2 tbsp water and steam for 2 min.
4. Drain and set aside.
5. Place salmon in a bowl and flake into small pieces.
6. Mix in basil leaves, tomatoes, mascarpone and mozzarella.
7. Add cabbage to the salmon mixture.
8. Season with salt and pepper.
9. Spoon the mixture into an ovenproof dish, top with butter and sprinkle with pine nuts.
10. Place in the oven for 10 min to brown the top of the dish.
11. Serve immediately accompanied by a mixed leaf salad dressed with oil and balsamic vinegar.

Spicy Mussels Rasam with Vegetable

aromatic hearty hot and sour South Indian broth

30 MIN   SERVES 2   NET CARB
14 g/serving

- 1 tbsp coconut oil
- 2 chillies, chopped
- 2 tsp coriander seeds
- 1 tsp fenugreek seeds
- 1 tsp black pepper
- 1 tsp black mustard seeds
- 1 clove garlic, chopped
- 8 curry leaves
- ½ tsp ground cumin
- 1 and ½ cm (½ inch) ginger, chopped
- 1 large tomato, chopped
- 1 tbsp tamarind paste
- 475 ml (2 cups) water
- 1 kg mussels
- handful coriander, chopped
- 1 lime, quartered
- 225g cauliflower rice (see p67)
- serve with Raita – 2 servings (see p39)

1 Prepare mussels – wash in cold water, discarding any that will not shut.

2 Set aside.

3 Fry chillies, coriander, fenugreek, black pepper and black mustard seeds in coconut oil for 1 min.

4 Add garlic, curry leaves, cumin, ginger, tomato, tamarind paste and water.

5 Bring to boil and simmer for 15 min.

6 Make cauliflower rice, and set aside.

7 When the broth mixture is ready, add mussels, cover the pan with a lid and steam for 4 min until mussels have opened.

8 Discard any that are not open.

9 Add cauliflower rice to the mixture and allow to heat through for 1 min.

10 Serve immediately.

11 Garnish with coriander and lime wedges.

12 Serve Raita on the side.

Indian Fish Curry

spices dance in your mouth

15 MIN   **SERVES 2**   **NET CARB**
11 g/serving

- 3 cloves garlic, chopped
- 3 cm (1 inch) ginger, chopped
- 1 green chilli, deseeded and chopped
- 110g (½ cup) tomatoes
- 15g onion (1 tbsp), chopped
- 1 tbsp coconut oil
- 1 tsp each ground coriander, ground cinnamon, ground fennel, ground cardamom, ground cumin and turmeric powders
- 225g (1 cup) coconut cream
- ½ tsp salt
- 225g white fish, chopped in large chunks
- 1 lime, juiced
- large handful coriander (cilantro), chopped
- cauliflower rice, 225g (1 cup) (see p67)

1 Prepare cauliflower rice.
2 Blend garlic, ginger, chilli and tomatoes until smooth.
3 Fry onion in coconut oil for 2 min.
4 Add spices and fry for 15 to 20 seconds.
5 Add coconut cream, season with salt.
6 Add fish and simmer for 4 or 5 min until just cooked.
7 Stir in lime juice, and add ¾ chopped coriander.
8 Garnish with remaining coriander.
9 Serve with cauliflower rice.

TIP | Canned coconut cream provides a smooth rich cream and water combo for recipes. The contents have to be well mixed (i.e. both cream and water). The mixture imparts a creamy goodness to all curries and sauces.

Prawn (Shrimp) Chow Mein

a classic Chinese dish

2H 10MIN   SERVES 2   NET CARB
13 g/serving

- 225g (1 cup) prawns (shrimps)
- 1 tbsp soy sauce
- 1 tbsp oyster sauce
- 2 tbsp vegetable stock
- 1 tsp sesame oil
- black pepper
- 1 tbsp coconut oil
- 2 cloves garlic, chopped
- 2.5 cm (1 inch) fresh ginger, chopped
- 110g (½ cup) mangetout (snap peas)
- 55g (¼ cup) carrot, shredded
- 110g (½ cup) beansprouts
- 4 salad onions, sliced
- zoodles (see p69)

1 Marinade prawns in soy sauce/oyster sauce/stock/ sesame oil and pepper for at least 2 hours.
2 Make zoodles and set aside.
3 Heat coconut oil in a wok, fry prawns and transfer to a plate.
4 Add garlic and ginger, stir fry for 1 min.
5 Add mangetout and carrot.
6 Stir fry for 3 min.
7 Add bean sprouts then re-add shrimps.
8 Serve immediately with zoodles and garnish with salad onion.

TIP | Traditional noodles are very high in carbs.

Lobster Risotto

a low-carb version of a traditional rice dish

10 MIN   SERVES 2   NET CARB
                                  15 g/serving

- 225g (1 cup) lobster meat, cooked
- 225g (1 cup) cauliflower rice (see p67)
- 15g (1 tbsp) shallots, finely sliced
- 2 garlic cloves, chopped
- 2 tbsp butter
- 30g (2 tbsp) Parmesan, grated
- 1 salad onion, chopped
- 2 tbsp mascarpone
- fish stock if required
- bunch basil leaves, chopped
- 1 lemon, wedges
- salt and pepper

1. Prepare cauliflower rice and set aside.
2. Fry shallots in butter, adding garlic after 1 min.
3. Add Parmesan, salad onion and basil.
4. Season with pepper.
5. Add lobster and cauliflower rice.
6. Add mascarpone and stir vigorously to meld all flavours together.
7. If required, add a little fish stock to further moisten.
8. Adjust seasoning and serve immediately.
9. Garnish with basil and lemon wedges.

Prawn (Shrimp) Stir Fry with Pine Nuts

a speedy one-pan recipe

20 MIN   **SERVES 2**   **NET CARB**
14 g/serving

- 225g (1 cup) broccoli, florets
- 1 tbsp coconut oil
- 30g (2 tbsp) pine nuts
- 1 clove garlic, sliced
- 4 salad onions, chopped
- 1 fresh red chilli, chopped
- 5 cm (2 inch) ginger, chopped
- 1 red pepper, sliced,
- 1 yellow pepper, sliced
- 170g (¾ cup) prawns (shrimp), cooked
- 110g (½ cup) bean sprouts
- 1 tbsp soy sauce
- 1 tbsp fish sauce
- 2 tbsp dry sherry
- 1 tsp sesame oil
- 1 lime, quartered

1. Stir fry broccoli with coconut oil in a wok for 1 min, season with salt and pepper, add 1 tbsp water and steam for 2 min.
2. Remove and set aside.
3. Dry roast nuts in a pan for a few seconds and set aside.
4. Fry garlic, onions, red chilli and ginger in the wok for 2 min.
5. Stir in peppers, prawns (shrimp) and bean sprouts.
6. Add soy, fish sauce, sherry and sesame oil.
7. Re-add broccoli.
8. Serve immediately, garnished with pine nuts and lime quarters.

Fish Jalfrezi

easy and healthy stir fry

20 MIN   SERVES 1   NET CARB
6 g/serving

- 225g (1 cup) white fish, bite-sized pieces
- 45g (3 tbsp) butter/ghee
- 2 tsp ground cumin
- 1 tsp ground coriander
- 2 red chilli, deseeded and diced
- 15g (1 tbsp) onion, diced
- 2 cloves garlic, chopped
- 1 cm (½ inch) ginger, chopped
- 1 medium tomato, chopped
- 55g (¼ cup) red or yellow pepper, sliced
- ½ tsp ground turmeric
- 1 green chilli, chopped
- handful fresh coriander (cilantro), chopped
- 150g (⅔ cup) spinach
- 2 tbsp yoghurt

1 Cut fish into bite-sized pieces.
2 Fry cumin, coriander and red chilli in butter.
3 Add onion and garlic and fry for 2 min.
4 Add ginger, tomato, peppers, turmeric and green chilli.
5 Fry for a further 2 min.
6 Add fish, season with salt and cook for 15 min.
7 Add 2 tbsp water if required.
8 Garnish with coriander.
9 Serve with spinach and yoghurt on the side.

> **TIP**
> Fry spinach in olive oil seasoned with salt and pepper. Then add 2 tbsp water and steam for 2 min. Serve immediately.

Bouillabaisse

traditional Provençal fish stew served with creamy cauliflower mash: full of flavour and nourishment

30 MIN   **SERVES 1**   **NET CARB**
14 g/serving

- 2 tbsp olive oil
- 15g (1 tbsp) shallot, chopped
- 2 cloves garlic, chopped
- ½ head of fennel, chopped
- 1 tsp each of thyme, marjoram and tarragon
- 45 ml (3 tbsp) dry white wine
- 90 ml (6 tbsp) fish stock
- 110g (½ cup) tomato, chopped
- 1 tsp tomato paste
- ½ red pepper, diced
- 1 strip orange peel
- pinch of saffron and chilli
- ½ lemon, juiced
- 1 whole white fish, filleted
- 110g prawns (shrimp)
- 55g (¼ cup) calamari (squid), rings
- handful of mussels
- salt and pepper
- cauliflower mash (see p71)

1. Make cauliflower mash.
2. Fry shallots and garlic in olive oil
3. Add fennel and herbs.
4. Add wine, stock, tomatoes, tomato paste and red pepper.
5. Stir all ingredients.
6. Add orange peel, saffron, chilli and lemon juice.
7. Stir for 2 min.
8. Add prawns, calamari, fish and mussels.
9. Cook for a few minutes.
10. Season with salt and pepper.
11. Serve with cauliflower mash.

Quick recipe

Prepare your own fish stock (photo left). Add fish carcass, assorted vegetables and herbs, water and a splash of wine, salt and pepper.
Cook for 40 min and strain.

Cambodian Fish Amok

supremely delicate flavour

25 MIN   SERVES 2   NET CARB
9 g/serving

Main dish

- 225g (1 cup) firm white fish, cut in small chunks
- 1 tbsp coconut oil
- 1 tbsp fish sauce
- 2 star anise
- 1 kaffir lime leaf, chopped
- 225 ml (1 cup) coconut cream (can)
- 1 egg, beaten lightly
- handful of coriander, chopped
- 225g (1 cup) spinach
- 1 tbsp olive oil
- salt; lemon or lime, quartered

Curry paste

- 2 lemongrass stalks, chopped
- 1 clove garlic, chopped
- 15g (1 tbsp) shallots, chopped
- 1 tsp turmeric
- ½ tsp dried red chillies
- 1 cm (½ inch) ginger, chopped
- 1 kaffir lime leaf, chopped
- 30g (2 tbsp) pine nuts

1. Make the curry paste: place lemongrass, garlic, shallots, turmeric, red chilli, ginger, kaffir lime leaf, pine nuts, salt and 3 tbsp coconut cream into a food processor.
2. Blend until smooth.
3. Heat coconut oil in a frying pan, add the curry paste and fry gently for 2 min.
4. Stir continuously.
5. Add fish sauce, salt, star anise, kaffir lime leaf and the rest of the coconut milk.
6. Remove from heat and, when cool, stir in beaten egg.
7. Add fish and herbs.
8. Cook on very low heat for 12 to 15 min until the custard is just set and the fish is cooked.
9. In a separate pan, fry spinach in olive oil.
10. Add 1 tbsp water and steam for 1 min.
11. Season with salt.
12. Serve fish with spinach on the side and garnish with lemon or lime quarters.

Hot and Sour Calamari (Squid)

served with chilli, mint and coriander salad
just mouthwatering

10 MIN **SERVES 2** **NET CARB** 4 g/serving

- 225g (1 cup) calamari (squid), cut in rings
- 1 tbsp coconut oil
- 1 gem lettuce, shredded
- 1 salad onion, halved and shredded
- handful mint, chopped
- handful coriander (cilantro), chopped

Dressing
- 1 and ½ tbsp lime juice
- 1 and ½ tbsp fish sauce
- 1 tbsp dry sherry
- ½ red chilli, chopped
- 1 clove garlic, chopped
- 1 cm (¼ inch) ginger, chopped
- 1 lemongrass stalk, finely chopped
- 1 kaffir lime leaf, finely shredded

1 Lightly fry the squid in oil for 3 or 4 min.
2 Mix dressing ingredients in a bowl.
3 Scatter lettuce, salad onion and herbs on a plate.
4 Mix squid and dressing together and spoon over salad.
5 Serve immediately.

Baked Sardines

such a simple nutritious dish

20 MIN   SERVES 2   NET CARB   175°C
                                  4 g/serving   (350°F)

- 8 sardines, gutted
- 2 tbsp olive oil
- 4 cloves garlic, chopped
- salt and pepper
  Salad
- 1 gem lettuce, shredded
- 6 baby tomatoes, halved
- 2 tbsp olive oil
- 1 tbsp balsamic vinegar

1 Make the salad and set it aside.
2 Place sardines on a baking tray.
3 Baste with olive oil.
4 Scatter garlic over sardines.
5 Bake for 15 min.
6 Season with salt and pepper.
7 Serve immediately with lettuce and tomato salad, dressed with olive oil and balsamic vinegar.

White Fish with Herby Wine Sauce

simply delicious and so nutritious

40 MIN **SERVES 2** **NET CARB**
6 g/serving

- 2 tsp fresh rosemary, chopped
- 2 tsp fennel stalks, chopped
- handful coriander (cilantro), chopped
- 2 tbsp white wine
- zest of half a lemon
- 1 clove garlic, chopped
- 90ml (6 tbsp) olive oil
- 1 bay leaf
- 225g (1 cup) white fish fillets
- 2 tbsp cream
- salt and black pepper
- 250g green vegetables of your choice

1 Blend herbs, wine, lemon zest, garlic and 50ml olive oil.
2 Place fish fillets in a dish and cover with the herb mixture for 30 min.
3 Fry fish and herb mixture in the remainder of the oil until cooked.
4 Add cream and seasoning and heat through.
5 Serve with green vegetables.

Tuna Steaks with Olives and Saffron

packed with vitamins and omega-3

50 MIN   **SERVES 2**   **NET CARB 5 g/serving**   **200°C (400 F)**

- 2 x 150g (5.2 oz) tuna steaks
- 15g (1 tbsp) shallot, chopped
- 1 clove garlic, chopped
- 3 tbsp olive oil
- pinch saffron
- 2 tbsp white wine
- 4 tbsp chicken stock
- 20g small black olives
- ½ lemon, thinly sliced
- handful parsley, chopped
- salt and black pepper
- roasted radishes (see p119)

1. Prepare radishes and place in the oven for 45 min: 30 min at 200°C, then turn the heat down to 175°C (350°F) for 15 min when adding tuna.
2. While the radishes are in the oven, season tuna with salt and pepper.
3. Fry shallots and garlic in olive oil, then add fish and brown on both sides, 2 min each side.
4. Soak saffron in wine for a few minutes.
5. Pour saffron mixture and stock into the pan.
6. Stir.
7. Add black olives and lemon slices.
8. Simmer gently for 2 or 3 min.
9. Transfer all ingredients to an ovenproof dish and place in the oven alongside the radishes.
10. Turn the temperature down to 175°C (350°F) for 12 to 15 min.
11. Place fish on warm plates.
12. Transfer sauce to pan and quickly reduce over high heat.
13. Spoon sauce over fish and garnish with parsley.
14. Serve with roasted radishes.

Barbecued Trout

great for a summer day

25 MIN   SERVES 2   NET CARB
8 g/serving   GRILL

- Aioli (see p33), use 2 tbsp
- 2 small trout, gutted
- 3 tbsp olive oil
- 1 lemon, zest and juice
- 1 clove garlic, chopped
- 30g (2 tbsp) butter
- 300g, 2 red peppers, halved and deseeded
- salt and pepper

1 Make Aioli.
2 Coat trout skin with olive oil and place in griddle on BBQ.
3 Turn fish regularly until cooked (5 to 10 mins in total depending on size).
4 Place red peppers on griddle and roast all around until skins are blackened.
5 Remove fish from the grill.
6 Plate fish and cover with lemon juice, zest, butter and Aioli.
7 Season with salt and pepper and serve with red peppers (roughly sliced).

Mackerel Recheado

deliciously simple with a hint of Goa

30 MIN　　　**SERVES 2**　　　**NET CARB**
11 g/serving

- Masala paste (see p31)
- Raita (see p39), use 2 servings with this dish
- 2 whole mackerel or 4 fillets
- 2 tbsp olive oil
- salt
- lemon, wedges

Tomato salad
- 200g tomatoes, sliced
- 15g (1 tbsp) shallots, sliced
- 1 tbsp coriander (cilantro), chopped
- ¼ tsp cumin
- pinch ground chilli
- 1 tbsp white wine vinegar
- salt and pepper

1　Make Masala paste.
2　Spread 1 tbsp masala paste inside each mackerel.
3　Tie fish to hold paste inside.
4　Make Raita and set aside.
5　Make tomato salad in layers, tomato first then shallot, topped by coriander.
6　Sprinkle cumin and chilli over top.
7　Add wine vinegar and seasoning.
8　Leave flavours to meld.
9　Fry mackerel for at least 3 mins on each side until golden brown.
10　Serve mackerel with tomato salad.
11　Add Raita as a side dish and lemon wedges

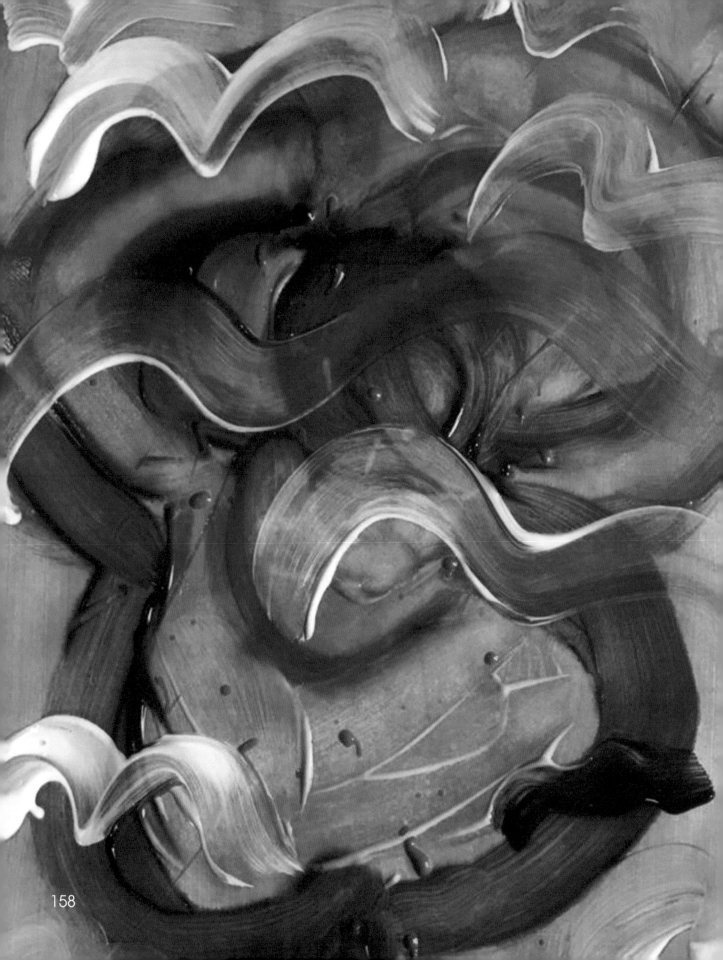

Acknowledgements

On completion of our second book, *Eat Your Way to Health: Recipes for Success,* we were asked the question 'Have you any thoughts on writing a pescatarian cookbook?' It was a good question, so we thought it over and decided that, yes, we would like to add one to our collection. We love fresh fish and vegetables, so it was a joy to work on such a variety of recipes. Moreover, we are very blessed to have an excellent local selection of both fresh vegetables and fish.

Issy Warrack

Estrelita van Rensburg

About the authors

Growing up on two different continents – one in Scotland and the other in South Africa – gave the authors two different perspectives on fresh local foods. Their food choices in early life were dictated by the fresh meat, fruit and vegetables available from local farms. However, each of them encountered new culinary experiences with seafood when they moved to the coast on their respective continents: Edinburgh, Scotland and Cape Town, South Africa. The fish species available in each country is, of course, totally different, but the variety and quality of fish protein available was a common interest factor. This was complemented by a greater array of fresh vegetables in the markets than had been part of their childhood diet and which contributed to the composition of this book.

Printed in Great Britain
by Amazon

65609483R00089